Nanabette's Cats

©2021 by Kelley Sewell
This is a work of fiction. Names, characters, organizations, places, events, and incidents are either products of the author's imagination or are used fictitiously.
All rights reserved. No part of this publication may be reproduced or transmitted in any form or by any means, electronic or mechanical, including photography, recording, or any information storage and retrieval system, without permission in writing from the author.

Requests for permission to make copies of any part of the work should be mailed to the following address: kelley@kelleysewell.com

For Betty and Joe Snyder—who open their hearts and home to all who come knocking or scratching.

This is Nanabette. She lives with Joe-Pa and their three cats—Boots, Scruffles, and Monkeytail.

Nanabette takes care of everyone in the family. She cooks all the meals and brushes the cats' fur every morning. She pours each one of them a bowl of milk at breakfast time and makes sure Boots gets medicine for his tummy. She also makes sure Joe-Pa has slices of fresh lemon for his iced tea and hot peppers for his salad.

One day, Nanabette said, "I have a big announcement. I'm going to visit my brother, Bobby George, in Texas. I haven't seen him in a long time and he needs my help."

"But who will feed us?" asked Monkeytail.

"Who will give us our bowls of milk?" asked Scruffles.

"Who will give me my tummy medicine?" asked Boots.

"And who will slice my lemons for my iced tea and my hot peppers for my salad?" asked Joe-Pa.

"You are all going to be just fine. Joe-Pa will take care of you cats. Now, the rains are coming soon, so please be sure to stay warm and dry. And please, kitties, do not scratch up Joe-Pa's recliner chair while I'm away."

With that, Nanabette patted each one of them on the head and was out the door to catch her plane.

Joe-Pa fed the cats every day and gave them their bowls of milk right on time. Boots took his medicine every morning. And sure enough, the rain started to fall just as Nanabette said. The cats stared out the window and watched the raindrops water Nanabette's flower garden.

"Nanabette used to brush my fur coat everyday. No one's doing that," said Scruffles sadly.

"Nanabette used to sing to me when my tummy hurt," Boots cried.

"Nanabette used to let me sleep on her bed," Monkeytail meowed loudly, curling up his tail into a tight ball.

"She did?!" Scruffles and Boots looked at each other in surprise.

Joe-Pa folded his arms and looked at the sad kitties.

"I miss Nanabette, too. I don't have anyone to talk to except you cats. It is important that Nanabette spend time with her brother. She does so much for all of us so let's get along and help each other out. That is what Nanabette would want." Joe-Pa wanted to do something nice to surprise Nanabette when she returned home.

The cats figured Joe-Pa was right. They should all get along and help each other, but it was lonely without Nanabette.

One night, the phone rang and woke everyone up.

"Maybe it's Nanabette!" Scruffles whispered to the others.

Joe-Pa answered the phone. It was Nanabette!

"Joe-Pa, I'm sorry, but I have to stay at my brother's house another week," Nanabette said. "I will be back next Saturday."

Joe-Pa missed Nanabette but it was important that she spend time with her brother. It was only one more week. Joe-Pa tried hard to think of a surprise for her when she returned home.

But the cats were not so understanding. "One more week?!" cried Boots.

"What if she calls again to tell us it will be another week? Or another month?" wondered Scruffles.

"There is only one thing to do. We have to go find Nanabette," said Monkeytail.

"Go find her? How are we going to get to Texas?" Boots raised his eyebrows.

"I know!" Scruffles had an idea. "We will hop on a train."

"I've never been on a train before." Monkeytail covered his eyes with his paws.

"There's nothing to it," said Scruffles. "I've been on trains lots of times. I'll show you the way."

Monkeytail had the job of carrying the kitty chow for the trip in his knapsack.

Scruffles led the way in the rain to the train station where they waited for an open train car.

"There's one!" yelled Scruffles. "Go! Go! Go!"

The cats ran as fast as they could alongside the train, but the rain made the ground slick. With a leap, Scruffles nearly slipped, but luckily landed on one of the railcars. "Come on, come on!" he called to the others.

Boots jumped with all his might and landed right next to Scruffles.

Monkeytail had fallen a little behind with the weight of the knapsack, which was getting heavy with rainwater.

"You must run as fast as you can, Monkeytail!" Scruffles cried.

"Think of how happy Nanabette will be to see us!" Boots cheered.

Monkeytail thought how nice it would be to curl up on Nanabette's lap again. Suddenly, he had a burst of energy and ran faster than ever before.

Scruffles grabbed Monkeytail by his wet fur and pulled him to the train car, but Monkeytail lost hold of the knapsack. Boots was quick and scooped it up before it hit the railroad track. What a close call!

The train ride was long, but the thought of seeing Nanabette made it go a little faster.

Many hours later they arrived in Texas. They hopped off the train as it came to a stop. The weather was sunny and hot, not rainy and wet like it was when they left California.

"How will we find Nanabette? We don't know where her brother lives," Monkeytail frowned.

Out of nowhere, a big cowboy cat with a shiny star on his collar showed up.

"You cats don't look like you're from around these parts. What brings you to my town?"

"We are looking for our Nanabette. She's staying with her brother, Bobby George. Can you help us find her?" Boots asked.

The cowboy cat looked down at Boots' boots. "We don't usually help out city slickers around here, but you are wearing a nice pair of boots, so I guess you're OK. I'll help you, but it's going to cost you."

"Anything!" cried Monkeytail.

"That's a nice knapsack you got there. I can smell it's full of kitty chow. I reckon that would be payment enough."

"But that's all our food!" cried Scruffles.

"Do you want to find your Nanabette or not?" the cowboy cat asked.

"We need to eat too, you know! Who knows how long it will take us to find Nanabette!" Scruffles was ready to pounce on the cowboy cat. Monkeytail had to hold him back.

The cowboy cat turned and started to walk away.

"Your choice, boys. I've got plenty of canned food at home. I don't need your kitty chow." The cowboy cat waved his tail back and forth as he walked away.

"Wait! Wait!" Boots called after him. "You got yourself a deal. You can have all our kitty chow."

The cowboy cat turned around. "At least one of you has some sense. No surprise it's the one with the boots."

"How do we know you'll take us to the right place?" Scruffles asked.

"I know all the cats around for miles," said the cowboy cat. "We hear Miss Kitty just got a visit from an Aunt Nanabette who lives in California. Rumor has it, she just might go back home with her. Could this be the Nanabette you're looking for?"

"Why, yes! I'm sure it is! Please Mr. Cowboy Cat, get us there as fast as you can!" cried Monkeytail.

The cowboy cat showed them the way to an underground tunnel guarded by a tough cat named Gato.

"Show these cats the way to Miss Kitty's house. They're looking for their Nanabette."

"Oh, yes, we know all about her. All the cats in town have been over to visit! It's going to be a long journey my friends, but we will get you to your Nanabette."

Back at home, Joe-Pa worried about the cats. They had been gone for three days. How would he explain this to Nanabette? He had to call and let her know.

"Oh no!" Nanabette cried. "Did you feed them?" she asked.

"Yes," said Joe-Pa.

"Did you give them water and their bowls of milk?" asked Nanabette.

"Yes," said Joe-Pa.

"Well, did you give Boots his medicine?" asked Nanabette.

"Yes," said Joe-Pa again. "I did everything you asked me to."

"I'll be coming home in a few more days. Hopefully, they'll come back before I get home."

That night, Nanabette could not sleep. She kept thinking about Scruffles, Boots, and Monkeytail. Miss Kitty followed her as she walked back and forth across the wood floor. If only she could tell Nanabette that her cats were on their way to see her!

Scruffles, Boots, and Monkeytail traveled all night. They finally arrived as the sun started to rise.

"This is the end of the line, Muchachos," announced Gato. "This is Miss Kitty's place. Good luck, Amigos."

"Gracias!" They all thanked Gato and ran toward the house.

Miss Kitty could hear them coming up the steps and started scratching wildly at the front door.

"Do you need to go out, Miss Kitty?" Nanabette asked.

Nanabette opened the door and suddenly Boots, Scruffles, and Monkeytail ran into the house and jumped into her arms.

"How did you find me?" Nanabette cried.

Nanabette was so happy. "I bet you are all starving. Let's find you something to eat."

The cats purred loudly as they ate their food.

"Nanabette knows just how I like my breakfast," Scruffles smiled.

"And she knows just how I like my milk," Monkeytail said, curling up his tail.

"And my medicine doesn't even taste bad when Nanabette gives it to me," purred Boots.

Nanabette called Joe-Pa to let him know the cats were all safe and would be coming home with her on the plane.

Joe-Pa couldn't wait for Nanabette to come home. He had thought of the perfect surprise for her and the cats. He started working on it the night before. It was a playhouse for Monkeytail, Boots, and Scruffles with carpet, stairs, and even windows. Nanabette would be so happy the cats could have a cozy place to keep them warm and dry. They would have a proper place to scratch, tumble, and play too.

Finally, it was time for Nanabette to leave for the airport and fly home. All the cats were ready to go in their carriers.

Nanabette and her brother did not see Miss Kitty sneak into one of the carriers with Monkeytail.

"Shhhh," Miss Kitty whispered. "Please don't tell anyone. I just want to come out to California for a little visit." Miss Kitty curled up at the back of the carrier behind Monkeytail so no one could see her.

After Nanabette's plane arrived at the airport, she placed the three cat carriers in her car and drove home. All the cats slept soundly from the long airplane trip.

Joe-Pa helped bring the carriers and Nanabette's suitcase into the house. He was so happy she and the cats were home safe and sound.

"I have something to show all of you," Joe-Pa said. "It's outside on the back patio. Follow me."

Nanabette, Monkeytail, Boots, and Scruffles all followed Joe-Pa to the back patio.

Meanwhile, Miss Kitty yawned and stretched after her nap inside Monkeytail's carrier. She stepped out and looked around. Where had everyone gone?

She heard voices coming from outside. She scampered into the kitchen and hopped up onto the counter to look out the window.

"A cat house?!" Nanabette squealed and put her hands on her cheeks. "What a perfect surprise! Thank you!" Nanabette gave Joe-Pa a big hug.

The cats immediately jumped through the open door into their new house and started running around.

Once Joe-Pa, Nanabette, and the cats came back into the house, Joe-Pa and Nanabette stopped in their tracks when they saw Miss Kitty. Joe-Pa rubbed his eyes to make sure he was seeing clearly.

"Another cat?" he asked. "Where did you come from?"

"I see we had a little stowaway. That's my brother's cat, Miss Kitty," Nanabette said. "Looks like I'll be making another trip to Texas!"

The End

About the Author

Kelley's passion for storytelling ignited as a kid during family vacations near majestic Mt. Shasta where she couldn't wait to entertain her twin nephews with her latest spooky tale around the campfire. Kelley loves writing all kinds of stories to this day and gains inspiration on long walks with her German shepherd, Apollo. Kelley calls northern California home where she lives with her husband and sons, Shawn and Cameron. Get in touch with Kelley at kelleysewell.com.